W9-ALG-854

A BEACON BIOGRAPHY

BRYCE HARPER

John Bankston

PURPLE TOAD
PUBLISHING

Printing   1   2   3   4   5   6   7   8   9

A Beacon Biography

Alexandria Ocasio-Cortez	Ellen DeGeneres	Meghan Markle
Angelina Jolie	Elon Musk	Michelle Obama
Anthony Davis	Ezekiel Elliott	Millie Bobby Brown
Ben Simmons	Gal Gadot	Misty Copeland
Big Time Rush	Harry Styles of One Direction	Mo'ne Davis
Bill Nye	Jennifer Lawrence	Muhammad Ali
Brie Larson	Joel Embiid	Neil deGrasse Tyson
Bryce Harper	John Boyega	Oprah Winfrey
Cam Newton	Keanu Reeves	Peyton Manning
Carly Rae Jepsen	Kevin Durant	Robert Griffin III (RG3)
Carson Wentz	Lorde	Scarlett Johansson
Chadwick Boseman	Malala	Stephen Colbert
Daisy Ridley	Markus "Notch" Persson,	Stephen Curry
Drake	Creator of Minecraft	Tom Holland
Ed Sheeran	Megan Rapinoe	Zendaya

Library of Congress Cataloging-in-Publication Data
Bankston, John.
  Bryce Harper / Written by: John Bankston
     p.cm.
Includes bibliographic references, glossary, and index.
ISBN 978-1-62469-519-3
         1. Harper, Bryce, 1992- —Juvenile literature. 2. Baseball players—United States Biography—Juvenile literature. 3. Washington Nationals (Baseball Team)—Juvenile Literature. 4. Phillies (Baseball Team)—Juvenile literature. I Series: A Beacon Biography.

GV865. H268 B36 2019
796.357092 B

Library of Congress Control Number: 2019949378

eBook ISBN: 9781624695216

ABOUT THE AUTHOR: John Bankston is the author of over 100 books for young readers, including biographies of Kevin Durant, Venus Williams, and Abby Wambach. Growing up, he loved watching the Red Sox play at Fenway Park in Boston, Massachusetts. He often attended games with both his parents and his grandparents. He lives in Miami Beach, Florida, with his ChiJack, Astronaut.

PUBLISHER'S NOTE: This story has not been authorized or endorsed by Bryce Harper.

CONTENTS

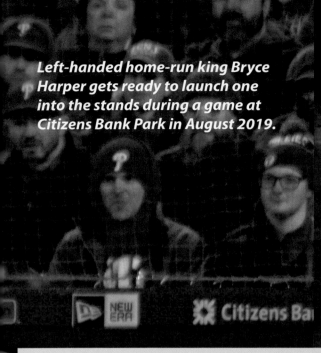

Chapter 1

Record Breaker

The bus driver stormed into the office. He was upset. Driving beside Las Vegas High School, he heard something hit his bus. He thought students were throwing balls at it.

The assistant principal raced to the baseball field. He "came up and stood behind the backstop, and he would not leave," the school's baseball coach, Sam Thomas, remembered. Finally the coach halted batting practice. "What's the matter?" he asked.

"I have a city bus driver in my office right now, and he's telling me that your kids have been throwing baseballs at his bus," the assistant principal replied.

"Did you explain to him that Bryce was hitting?" Thomas asked.

"I tried to, but he won't believe me."

Harper would become one of the highest-paid baseball players in the major leagues. As a high school athlete, he was already famous.

"We probably should have stopped traffic when he was hitting," Thomas admitted.[1]

It was 2008. Bryce Harper was a 15-year-old freshman. Already he was outplaying the seniors. The next year he'd grace the cover of *Sport Illustrated*.

The article described his longest home run as a freshman. The ball had sailed "over the right field fence, two trees, another fence, a sidewalk, five lanes of traffic on elevated South Hollywood Boulevard and yet another sidewalk, until it finally landed in the brown, undeveloped desert" to the right of Clark County Fire Station No. 31. From the batter's box to where it landed was 570 feet.[2]

Some questioned that record. Yet by the time the article came out, Bryce owned another one. In the 2009 Power Showcase, he competed in a home run derby at Tropicana Field in Tampa Bay, Florida. Pro players on the hometown Tampa Bay Rays or their opponents batted most of the home runs. Although he finished the competition in second place, Bryce would be number one in the record books. He hit the longest home run in Tropicana Field history: 502 feet.

Being the most famous player in high school baseball wasn't easy. When he picked up his bat, pitchers didn't want him to score. To keep Bryce from hitting a home run, they threw walks—balls far outside his strike zone. Recruiters didn't have a chance to see his skills. College recruiters often watch talented high school athletes. They help players get into top schools. This was different. The recruiters watching Bryce weren't from colleges. They were from Major League Baseball (MLB) teams. They wanted Bryce to turn pro.

Becoming a professional baseball player had been Bryce's goal for years. It began almost as soon as he picked up a bat. The dream was fed as he caught balls pitched by his older brother, when both Harpers played for the same high school just blocks from their home.

All-star outfielder Bryce Harper warms up with a teammate. Harper was the youngest player on the team.

The Las Vegas Strip's neon lights and 24-hour fun were a world away for one of the city's best-known athletes. Bryce Harper had a fairly normal childhood with hardworking parents who supported his dreams.

Always Youngest

Las Vegas, Nevada, is one of the most famous cities in the world. Constructed in the desert, it lies 270 miles from Los Angeles, California. Along the Las Vegas Strip, neon lights decorate hotels where adults can gamble, dance, or dine 24 hours a day. Families also visit, enjoying swimming pools and roller coasters. Over 42 million people came to Las Vegas in 2018. This city is where Bryce Harper grew up.[1]

Bryce Aron Max Harper was born on October 16, 1992. His mother, Sheri, was a paralegal. She helped lawyers write legal papers. Bryce's dad, Ron, was a steelworker. He helped build the new hotels sprouting regularly in Las Vegas. Talking about his dad, Bryce remembered, "He worked from two in the morning 'til one in the afternoon, he grinded every single day. It was take your lunch pail to work and do your job."[2]

As a little boy Bryce had one goal. He wanted to be better than his brother. Bryan was almost three years older. When Bryan was six, he joined a T-ball team. Bryce wanted to play with his brother, so he joined too. There aren't a lot of three-year-olds playing T-ball. Yet he kept up. Until he was in his 20s, Bryce was usually the youngest player on his team. "I love playing against the older guys," he admitted, "because I love showing up the older guys."[3]

Bryce threw with his right hand, but copied his brother's left-handed hitting style. Bryan and his teammates were not the only ones helping Bryce improve. Ron Harper had played baseball and football in high school. After a long day of work, he would coach his two sons. To help them get better at hitting and catching a baseball, he tossed sunflower seeds and bottle caps. Baseballs usually move in a straight line. Throwing things that don't move that way improved the Harper boys' skills.

One of the sport's all-time greats, Babe Ruth held the home-run record for nearly 40 years. Many believe Bryce will someday shatter Babe's record of 714 career runs.

Father and sons also worked on his hitting. Today Bryce's swing is often compared to legend Babe Ruth's. Often called the best baseball player of all time, Ruth hit over 700 home runs during his career.

"The full thing is God-given," Bryce explained. "I

No one made Bryce practice. He loved it, often hitting in batting cages during football season.

don't know how I got my swing or what I did. I know I worked every single day. I know I did as much as I could with my dad. . . . There was nothing really like, 'Oh, put your hands here.' It was, 'Where are you comfortable? You're comfortable here, hit from there.' "[4]

When Bryce was six, he played baseball at a youth camp. He was no longer hitting off a tee. Sam Thomas ran the camp. He never forgot the energetic blond boy who "had a way about him that said, 'I'm going to do it, and I'm going to do it better than everyone.' That's an age where you're happy if you can get a kid to wear catcher's gear. He wore it like a second skin."[5]

Bryce endured Nevada's hot, dry weather playing baseball in the shadow of Clark County's Frenchman Mountain.

Over a decade later, Thomas learned how skilled Bryce had become. Thomas was the baseball coach at Las Vegas High School. During winter holidays, he ran a competition for his best players. Both senior captains wanted Bryce on their team. There was one problem. Bryce was in junior high. Thomas decided to let him play. After Bryce's team won, the coach realized he was easily the best player on the field.

Thomas hoped Bryce would join his brother at L.V. High. Although top private schools recruited him, Bryce chose to attend the school a short walk from his house.

By then Bryce was no longer just playing locally. At nine, he had joined his first traveling team. These teams play baseball across the country. Parents can spend thousands of dallars for hotels and airfare. For Bryce, the teams covered his costs. Most years he played in over 100 games. He loved it. "Everything about it was great. I got to go places, meet people, play baseball against older kids and better competition. I had a great time,"[6] he said.

After a long weekend of playing baseball, he'd head to the batting cage. During football season, he worked on his batting skills—taking swings while wearing his padded football pants. He even slept with his bat.

Competing against players four years his senior wasn't enough. At 15, he was getting more walks than home runs. He wasn't able to play his best.

Kurt Stillwell was in the major leagues for 13 years. He scouted players for agent Scott Boras, who helped athletes get the best deals when they turn pro. Bryce was 14 when Stillwell started watching him play. He realized playing high school baseball wasn't just boring for Bryce, it was dangerous for the other players.

"He was too good for high school baseball . . . ," Stillwell remembered. "One day I was watching, and he hit a line drive past the shortstop, and the kid never reacted. He never saw it. Somebody was going to get hurt if he kept playing at that level."[7]

Stillwell and Boras had a plan. If it worked, while his classmates were graduating from high school, Bryce Harper would be turning pro.

Bryce was so talented he put other high school players in danger every time he hit the ball. When most teens were making prom plans, he was getting ready to turn pro.

Many high school stars struggle in college, but Bryce's career was rounding third and headed toward Major League Baseball.

Brothers in Bats

In 2008, sports agent Scott Boras landed a 10-year, $252 million deal for Alex Rodriguez. It was the richest deal in baseball. Like most of Boras's clients, the Yankees shortstop was in his twenties.

Boras remembers the call he got from Kurt Stillwell. "Kurt was rather nervous," said Boras. "He said, 'I need you to come see this kid right away.' . . . Kurt said this is kind of an unusual case because the kid is only 14 years old. My staff likes to play jokes on me. I thought this was one of them."[1]

When he visited Las Vegas High School, Boras realized Stillwell wasn't joking. Bryce Harper hit a home run off his very first pitch. Unfortunately, Bryce was walked his next nine times at bat. Boras agreed with Stillwell. Harper needed to play college baseball—the sooner the better. "They were walking him to death," Boras remembered. "We told him there would be no junior prom or senior prom, but high school baseball was not going to reward him anymore."[2]

Instead of taking classes, Bryce studied for his general equivalency diploma (GED). The GED test showed that he understood high school subjects. Meanwhile, he made the record books. Baseball America named him High School Player of the Year. Before Bryce, every Player

The Coyotes have had other players reach the majors, including pitcher Mike Dunn.

of the Year had been a senior. By then he was 6-foot-3 and weighed over 200 pounds. He no longer looked like a high school player.

He passed the GED in October of 2009 and enrolled at the College of Southern Nevada. A junior college, the CSN baseball team began in 2000. Just three years later, the team made history. On May 31, 2003, the CSN Coyotes won the National Junior College World Series. No other team had done that so quickly.

The team's head coach had known Bryce for years. "He's been hitting in our cages probably since he was six," Tim Chambers remembered. "I met his dad playing softball like 20 years ago. . . . [Bryce] was just kind of pudgy when he was younger, but when he was eight or nine you started to realize he was special because you just couldn't believe someone that young was hitting the ball that hard."[3]

Bryce had a lot of good reasons to play for CSN. He knew the coach, and the school was close to home. The team used wooden bats—just like Major League Baseball—partly because they make it harder to hit home runs. And he wouldn't be the only Harper on the team.

Bryan transferred to CSN from Cal State Northridge in California the help his brother deal with college life. Although Bryan was drafted after graduating high school, he decided to go to the university instead. "I don't have any regrets . . . ," he said. "I had to go to California on my own. I didn't know anybody. I had to pay my rent, pay bills and I learned a lot. It didn't work out on the field, so I went back to CSN."[4]

During his only year at CSN, Bryce hit 29 home runs. That was more than double the record of 12—which had happened when CSN players still hit with aluminum bats.

"We're 400 [feet] to center field with a 25-foot fence . . . ," Chambers explained. "I've seen six balls go over the scoreboard in center field and five of them were with aluminum and one of them was with wood, and that was Bryce's this year."[5]

Like almost every Major League Baseball player, Harper started in the minors. Here he's seen in uniform for the Hagerstown, Maryland, Suns.

Bryce had an amazing season. The year before, one MLB team was less successful. Playing in the nation's capital, the Washington Nationals attract a hometown crowd that includes U.S. Senators and reporters. During the first week, the team fell to five games behind the division leader. The team finished the season with only 59 wins, losing 103 games. It was the worst record by far for any team in Major League Baseball.

The bad record had a bright spot. The worst team gets to pick first in the next year's draft. Held every June, the draft is when MLB teams select top players. Months before, many predicted the Nationals would choose Bryce. When they did just that, he became the first number-one draft pick from a junior college. In August he signed a five-year contract with the team. It was for $9.9 million. He was paid $6 million immediately. Bryce was seventeen years old.

Before he was an adult, Harper became a millionaire, earning a $6 million signing bonus when he was drafted by the Nationals.

Just outside the batter's box, Bryce Harper stopped. He dropped his bat, bent down, and scooped up some dirt. He rubbed it into his palms. Bryce doesn't wear gloves. "He's got this thing for dirt," his mom explained when Bryce was a high school freshman.[1]

It was the April 2011 opening game and Bryce's first at-bat. He hit the ball into center field and made it to first base. His second hit was even shorter. He bunted.

After getting drafted, the former catcher became a right fielder in the Arizona Fall League. He also played with the Nationals during spring training. His new team was a Nationals farm team. The Hagerstown, Maryland, Suns played in the South Atlantic League in the lowest rank of minor league baseball: Class A. "Just another day in paradise," he joked after the game. "It's a blast. It's everything I've wanted to do."[2]

It was also very different from the major leagues. Major league players fly in private jets to away games. Minor leaguers take the bus. Major leaguers stay in hotels. Minor leaguers stay two-to-a-room in motels.

The biggest difference is money. The lowest paid Major League Baseball player earns over $500,000 a year. In the minor leagues,

Although he spent spring training with the Nationals, for the 2012 season Harper returned to the minor leagues.

players can earn just a few hundred dollars a week. Bryan Harper knows all about minor league life. Along with Bryce, he was one of 11 players drafted from the CSN baseball team. He signed with his brother's team as a 30th-round draft pick in 2011.

Eight years later, he was still a minor league player, making around $2,000 a month. This is about what someone makes as a cashier. "Nobody wants to truly come here. This isn't the first choice . . . ," Bryan admitted. "You have to love this game to be here doing what we're doing."[3]

On Independence Day, 2011, Bryce was sent to the Harrisburg, Pennsylvania, Senators. This team plays in the Class AA League. Less than six weeks later, he was sprinting from second to third base when he tore a hamstring. The coaches carried him off the field. His season was over.

In 2012, another player's injury sent Harper to "The Show"—the majors. He began the season playing for the AAA Syracuse, New York, Chiefs. After Ryan Zimmerman hurt his shoulder, Bryce was called up.

Some players weren't sure Harper was ready. Nationals right fielder Jayson Werth said, "[W]hen Bryce was younger he was kind of a knothead. I think the sense was that he just wasn't ready. He was just a kid, a child."[4]

On April 28, 2012, Harper played his first major league game. His first hit was a ground ball that was easily caught by the pitcher. His third time at bat, he got a double, hitting the ball off the top of the center-field wall. Later, his sacrifice fly gave the Nationals a 2-1 lead. Although they lost the game in extra innings, Werth became a believer. "He did that, and it was like, 'OK, he's here to stay.' "[5]

It wasn't easy being famous. In college and the minor leagues, Harper was booed. In the majors, he was hit. Playing against the Philadelphia Phillies on May 6, pitcher Cole Hamels hit Harper with the ball on purpose. Placed on the bases, Harper was able to eventually steal home base. No teenage player had done that since 1964. When he hit his first home run one week later, he was the youngest player to do so in almost twenty years.

Harper kept breaking records. He earned a spot on that year's National League All-Star team, the youngest player ever. The next year he hit two home runs during the team's opening game. He was the youngest major leaguer in history to do that.

Every player dreams of winning a World Series. After several horrible years, Nationals fans were excited just to see their team reach the playoffs. In 2011, the team almost had a winning record: 80 wins and 81 losses. The first year Harper played for the team, they won 98 games and lost only 64. The Nationals finished first in their division. The team finished either first or second in their division every year through 2018. The team won division titles in 2012, 2014, 2016, and 2017. Unfortunately they never reached the World Series.

By 2018, Harper was a free agent. He could go to any team that wanted him. The Nationals wanted him to stay. They also offered a deal that wouldn't finish paying out until Harper was almost 80. That was a long time to wait.

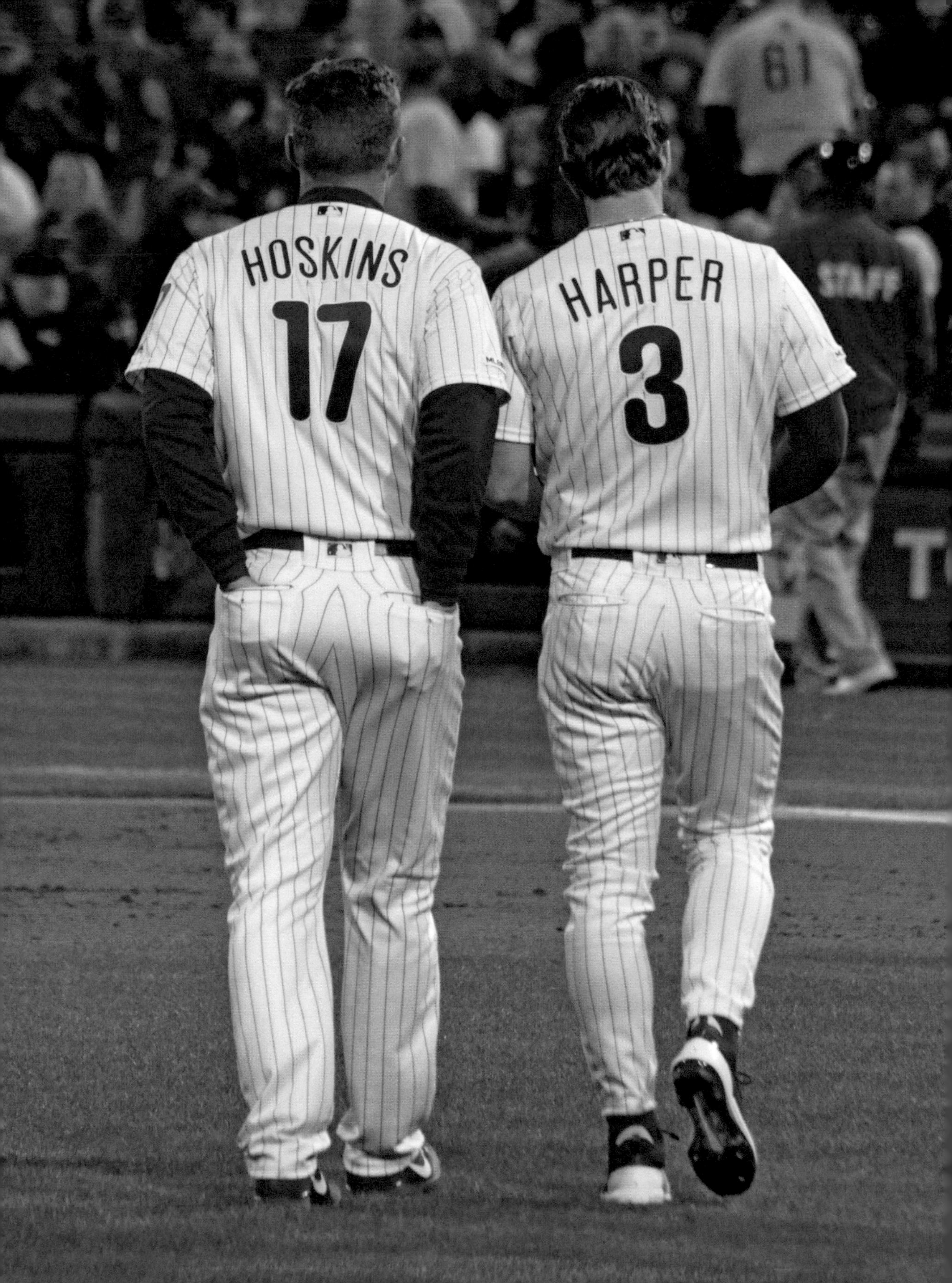
61
HOSKINS
17
HARPER
3
STAFF

Even top players need talented teammates and the double threat of a Hoskins-Harper combo should thrill Phillies fans for years.

World Series Dreams

In September 2018, the Nationals made him an offer. Harper wanted to stay. He wanted to play for the same team for at least ten years. In 2016 he'd married Kayla Varner, whom he'd met when they attended Las Vegas High School. He wanted to live in an East Coast city with her and raise a family.

The Nationals offered him a 10-year contract for $300 million. The last payment would be in 2052. He didn't sign. By January of 2019, lots of other teams wanted him. The Nationals made a new offer: 12 years for $250 million. The last payment wouldn't arrive until 2072.

Harper wasn't happy. "I don't want to be a guy that gets paid till I'm 65. That doesn't do it for me."[1]

There's a reason top athletes are paid millions. The team owners they work for make billions. A top player like Bryce Harper does more than win games. He puts fans in seats. They buy jerseys with his name. Cable sports channels air his games. "Of course, it would have been better to win a World Series," he admitted in 2019. "But other than that, I can't complain. The Nationals when I got there were worth $550 million, and they are worth $1.6 billion now."[2]

John Middleton was willing to spend more than $300 million to land Bryce Harper.

The Philadelphia Phillies were a lot like the Nationals before Harper arrived. In 2015, the team had the worst record in Major League Baseball. In 2018, it had a record of 80 wins and 82 losses. Team owner John Middleton wanted that to change. "I approach my job as a fan first," he explained. He told Scott Boras, "I've made enough money in my life. The only reason I'm talking to you about Bryce is that I believe he's a special player who can help us win and get my [World Series] trophy back."[3]

Middleton offered $330 million for 13 years. Every penny would be paid during that time. The Phillies were taking a chance on Harper. He was also taking a chance on them.

Even before his first at-bat, Harper changed things. Playing in South Philadelphia at Citizens Bank Park, the Phillies had won the World Series in 2008. Two years later, the team was tops in the National League for attendance. By 2018, they were 12th out of 15 teams. After announcing that Harper would play for them, the Phillies sold over 300,000 tickets in eight days. Their new player broke another record. No other jersey has ever sold more than Bryce Harper's did on its first day. His new number would be 3—the same as Babe Ruth's.

Taking his place in right field, Harper soon won over Phillies fans as he led the team to a first place start.

Yet playing against his former teammates was hard. On April 2, 2019, he listened as his name was announced. It sounded like every one of the 35,920 fans in Nationals Park was booing. "I heard the boos . . . ," Harper admitted. "I just tried to remember the city of Philadelphia is sitting back at home cheering and screaming and yelling at their TV happy as heck I'm a Philadelphia Phillie."[4]

Harper struck out his first two at-bats. In the eighth inning, the Phillies were ahead 6-0. Harper hit a 458-foot home run to right field. As he made his way toward home plate, he no longer heard boos. Most Nationals fans had left the park. Instead, visitors chanted over and over, "We got Harper!"[5]

Harper has embraced his new city and hopes to spend his baseball career in Philadelphia. Posing beside Pennsylvania Governor Tom Wolf and fellow Phillies player Andrew McCutchen, he joined them in celebrating the city's selection as host for the 2026 All-Star Game.

Married to his high school sweetheart Kayla Varner, Bryce hopes to raise a family in Philadelphia.

And he had them. Talking about his move to Philadelphia, Harper explained, "Understand that my family means the world to me—my wife, my mom and dad, everybody. I want to be able to sit there and have my kids grow up somewhere, not have to move around . . . this is an opportunity to play somewhere for 13 years and try to understand a city, and be into a city. . . . That's the greatest thing that could ever happen."[6]

Harper uses some of his money to share his love for the game. At his old high school, he donated money to help build Harper Field. The entrance is a black gate built partly with the wooden bats he used. Not far from Nationals Park, Harper helped pay for two different baseball complexes. At the dedication for the Bryce Harper All-Star Complex at Fred Crabtree Park, he looked out at the audience. Tears filled his eyes as he spotted his mom and dad in the crowd. "Growing up, that was

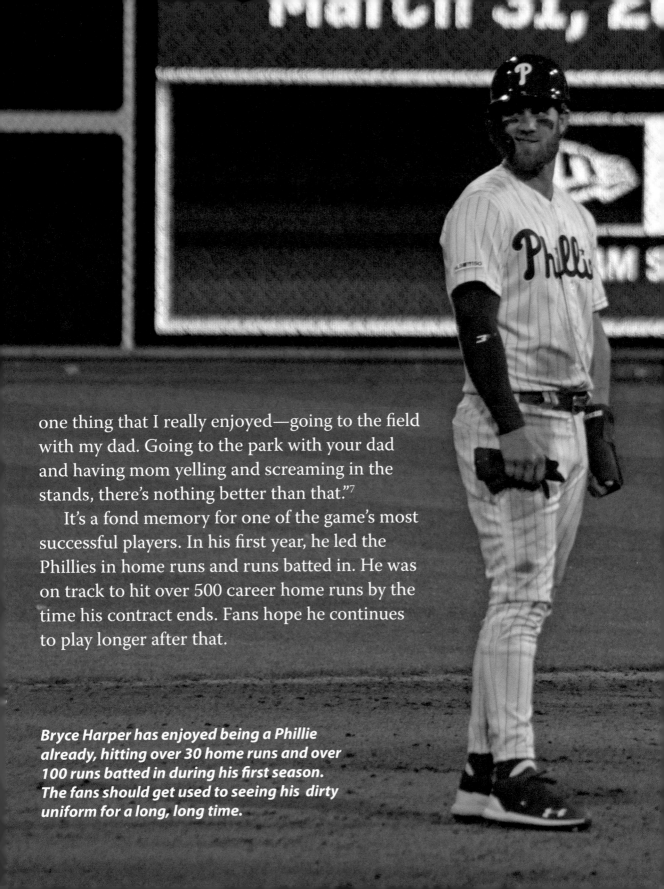

one thing that I really enjoyed—going to the field with my dad. Going to the park with your dad and having mom yelling and screaming in the stands, there's nothing better than that."[7]

It's a fond memory for one of the game's most successful players. In his first year, he led the Phillies in home runs and runs batted in. He was on track to hit over 500 career home runs by the time his contract ends. Fans hope he continues to play longer after that.

Bryce Harper has enjoyed being a Phillie already, hitting over 30 home runs and over 100 runs batted in during his first season. The fans should get used to seeing his dirty uniform for a long, long time.

1992   Bryce Aron Max Harper is born on October 16 in Las Vegas, Nevada.

1996   Bryce begins playing T-ball alongside six-year-old brother, Bryan.

2002   Bryce joins his first travel baseball teams. He will play all across the United States, competing in over 100 games a year.

2008   He plays in the Pan American Championships in Mexico as part of USA Baseball's Under-16 team. He is named Most Valuable Player after scoring four home runs.

2009   After earning his GED, he enrolls at the College of Southern Nevada (CSN).

2010   He plays baseball for the CSN Coyotes, breaking the school's home run record. He is picked first overall in the Major League Baseball draft, signing a five-year contract with the Washington Nationals worth $9.9 million.

2012   He plays his first major league game, hitting against the Dodgers in Los Angeles. Bryce is the youngest positional player in history when he joins the National League All-Star team.

2016   He and Kayla Varner marry.

2019   Harper signs the richest free-agent deal in baseball history with the Philadelphia Phillies for $330 million for 13 years.

AWARDS AND ACHIEVEMENTS

2018   Selected for his 7th MLB All-Star Game

2015   ESPN MLB Person of the Year

        National League Hank Aaron Award

        Silver Slugger Award

        National League Most Valuable Player

2012   National League Rookie of the Year

2010   Golden Spikes Award: Best Player in College Baseball.

2009   Baseball America High School Player of the Year.

MLB STATISTICS

Year	Team	G	AB	R	H	2B	3B	HR	RBI	BB	K	SB	AVG	OBP	SLG
2012	Was	139	533	98	144	26	9	22	59	56	120	18	.270	.340	.477
2013	Was	118	424	71	116	24	3	20	58	61	94	11	.274	.368	.486
2014	Was	100	352	41	96	10	2	13	32	38	104	2	.273	.344	.423
2015	Was	153	521	118	172	38	1	42	99	124	131	6	.330	.460	.649
2016	Was	147	506	84	123	24	2	24	86	108	117	21	.243	.373	.441
2017	Was	111	420	95	134	27	1	29	87	68	99	4	.319	.413	.595
2018	Was	159	550	103	137	34	0	34	100	130	169	13	.249	.393	.496
2019	Phi	157	573	98	149	36	1	35	114	99	178	15	.260	.372	.510
Career		1084	3879	708	1054	219	19	219	635	684	1012	90	.276	.385	.512

Chapter 1. Record Breaker

1. Brookover, Bob. "He Got His Start in Las Vegas. He Matured in D.C. Now, Bryce Harper Is 7th Ready to Shine in Philly." *Philadelphia Inquirer*, April 1, 2019.
2. Verducci, Tom. "Baseball's LeBron." *Sports Illustrated*, June 8, 2009.

Chapter 2. Always Youngest

1. "LVCVA Summary of Monthly Tourism Indicators for Las Vegas, NV: For Calendar Year 2018." Las Vegas Convention and Visitors Authority, April 23, 2019.
2. Kepner, Tyler. "His Deep Roots (and Deep Pockets) Lured Harper to the Phillies." *The New York Times*, March 24, 2019, p. 1(L).
3. Verducci, Tom. "Baseball's LeBron." *Sports Illustrated*, June 8, 2009.
4. Kilgore, Adam. "A Swing of Beauty." *The Washington Post*, n.d.
5. Brookover, Bob. "He Got His Start in Las Vegas. He Matured in D.C. Now, Bryce Harper Is Ready to Shine in Philly." *Philadelphia Inquirer*, April 1, 2019.
6. Verducci.
7. Brookover.

Chapter 3. Brothers in Bats

1. Brookover, Bob. "He Got His Start in Las Vegas. He Matured in D.C. Now, Bryce Harper Is Ready to Shine in Philly." *Philadelphia Inquirer*, April 1, 2019.
2. Ibid.
3. Glassey, Conor. "All About Bryce Harper." *Baseball America*, June 7, 2010.
4. Brookover, Bob. "Bryce Harper's Brother Makes $2,000 a Month Playing Independent Ball in Lancaster. He Loves It." *Philadelphia Inquirer*, May 23, 2019.
5. Glassey.

Chapter 4. The Show

1. Verducci, Tom. "Baseball's LeBron." *Sports Illustrated*, June 8, 2009.
2. Sheinin, Dave. "Harper Quietly Connects in First Minor League Outing." *The Washington Post*, April 8, 2011.
3. Brookover, Bob. "Bryce Harper's Brother Makes $2,000 a Month Playing Independent Ball in Lancaster. He Loves It." *Philadelphia Inquirer*, May 23, 2019.
4. Brookover, Bob. "He Got His Start in Las Vegas. He Matured in D.C. Now, Bryce Harper Is Ready to Shine in Philly." *Philadelphia Inquirer*, April 1, 2019.
5. Ibid.

Chapter 5. World Series Dreams

1. Svrluga, Barry. "How Bryce Harper Went from 'I'm Gonna Be a National' to 'We're Going to Philly.'" *The Washington Post*, April 1, 2019.
2. Brookover, Bob. "He Got His Start in Las Vegas. He Matured in D.C. Now, Bryce Harper Is Ready to Shine in Philly." *Philadelphia Inquirer*, April 1, 2019.
3. Kepner, Tyler. "His Deep Roots (and Deep Pockets) Lured Harper to the Phillies." *The New York Times*, March 24, 2019, p. 1(L).
4. Gardner, Steve. "Bryce Harper Booed Mercilessly by Nationals Fans, but Gets the Last Word." *USA Today*, April 2, 2019.
5. Dougherty, Jesse, and Bryan Flaherty. "'T-RA-I-T-O-R': Bryce Harper Booed in His First Trip Back to Nats Park." *The Washington Post*, April 2, 2019.
6. Kepner.
7. Silver, Zach. "Harper Dedicates Field Bearing his Name." Major League Baseball, July 16, 2018.

Books

Alexander, Andrea. *Sports Biographies: Bryce Harper*. Herndon, Virginia: Mascot Books, 2016.

Bodden, Valerie. *Bryce Harper (The Big Time)*. Mankato, Minnesota: Creative Education, 2013.

Fishman, Jon M. *Bryce Harper*. Minneapolis: Lerner, 2014.

Works Consulted

Adams, Katy, and Nikki Schwab. "Learning How to Be a Pro." *The Examiner* [Washington, D.C], April 7, 2011.

Bennett, Dashiel. "The 2009 Washington Nationals: A Season of Bigger Failure." *Deadspin*, September 17, 2009. https://deadspin.com/the-2009-washington-nationals-a-season-of-bigger-failu-5360945

Boswell, Thomas. "Washington Nationals Slugger Harper Is Happy, Healthy and Even Showing Some Maturity." *The Washington Post*, February 20, 2014.

Brookover, Bob. "Bryce Harper's Brother Makes $2,000 a Month Playing Independent Ball in Lancaster. He Loves It." *Philadelphia Inquirer*, May 23, 2019.

———. "He Got His Start in Las Vegas. He Matured in D.C. Now, Bryce Harper Is Ready to Shine in Philly." *Philadelphia Inquirer*, April 1, 2019.

Dougherty, Jesse, and Bryan Flaherty. " 'T-RA-I-T-O-R': Bryce Harper Booed in His First Trip Back to Nats Park." *The Washington Post*, April 2, 2019. https://www.washingtonpost.com/sports/2019/04/02/bryce-harper-nationals-park-reception-i-hope-i-get-great-one/?utm_term=.17f6c4431e78

"E-60: Bryce Harper." ESPN (video). http://youtu.be/ptrAnO5zcCk

Gardner, Steve. "Bryce Harper Booed Mercilessly by Nationals Fans, but Gets the Last Word." *USA Today*, April 2, 2019. https://www.usatoday.com/story/sports/mlb/2019/04/02/bryce-harper-philadelphia-phillies-washington-nationals/3347304002/

Glassey, Conor. "All About Bryce Harper." Baseball America, June 7, 2010. https://www.baseballamerica.com/stories/all-about-bryce-harper/

Janes, Chelsea. "Nationals' Bryce Harper Is about to Step into the Storm That's Been Brewing His Entire Life." *The Washington Post*, March 28, 2018.

Kepner, Tyler. "Harper Brushes Off the Future, and the Past." *New York Times*, February 2, 2018, p. B7(L).

———. "His Deep Roots (and Deep Pockets) Lured Harper to the Phillies." *The New York Times*, March 24, 2019, p. 1(L).

———. "Thwarted by One Shift, Harper Has His Eyes on Another." *The New York Times*, July 17, 2018, p. B5(L).

Kilgore, Adam. "A Swing of Beauty." *The Washington Post*, n.d. http://www.washingtonpost.com/wp-srv/special/sports/bryce-harper-swing-of-beauty/?noredirect=on

Levin, Arthur. "Could You Handle the Stratosphere's Thrill Rides?" *Tripsavvy*, January 6, 2018. https://www.tripsavvy.com/stratospheres-thrill-rides-4118941

"LVCVA Summary of Monthly Tourism Indicators for Las Vegas, NV: For Calendar Year 2018." Las Vegas Convention and Visitors Authority, April 23, 2019. https://assets.simpleviewcms.com/simpleview/raw/upload/v1/clients/lasvegas/Year_to_Date_Summary_for_2018_5ac99598-ba25-4773-9b75-8efc66ba23e1.xlsx

"No. 1 Pick in Baseball Is Sent to the Minors, for Now." *The New York Times*, March 12, 2011.

"Number of Visitors to Las Vegas in the United States from 2000 to 2018 (in Millions)." Statista. https://www.statista.com/statistics/221042/visitors-to-las-vegas/

Schwarz, Alan. "At 17, Baseball's Next Sure Thing: Bryce Harper." *The New York Times*, May 15, 2010. https://www.nytimes.com/2010/05/16/sports/baseball/16nationals.html

Sheinin, Dave. "Harper Is Experiencing Some Minor Bumps in the Early Going." *The Washington Post*, April 16, 2011, p. D.5.

———. "Harper Quietly Connects in First Minor League Outing." *The Washington Post*, April 8, 2011.

Silver, Zach. "Harper Dedicates Field Bearing His Name." Major League Baseball, July 16, 2018. https://www.mlb.com/news/bryce-harper-dedicates-his-own-field-c286108282

Svrluga, Barry. "How Bryce Harper Went from 'I'm Gonna Be a National' to 'We're Going to Philly.'" *The Washington Post*, April 1, 2019.

Verducci, Tom. "Baseball's LeBron." *Sports Illustrated*, June 8, 2009. https://www.si.com/vault/2009/06/08/105822135/baseballs-lebron

On the Internet

Bryce Harper:

https://www.baseball-reference.com/players/h/harpebr03.shtml

http://www.espn.com/mlb/player/_/id/30951/bryce-harper

https://www.mlb.com/player/bryce-harper-547180

Learn about Babe Ruth, the player Bryce Harper is often compared to:

http://www.baberuth.com

GLOSSARY

contract (KON-tract)—A legal agreement.

draft (DRAFT)—The selection of players for a team.

professional (proh-FEH-shuh-nul)—A person who is paid for an activity or skill.

recruiter (ree-KROO-ter)—A person hired to find the best players for a college or professional team.